FULL
Rockets, Bells & Poetry

FULL

Rockets, Bells & Poetry

Warren Bluhm

warrenbluhm.com

FULL
Rockets, Bells & Poetry
© 2021 Warren Bluhm
All rights reserved

Cover image Space Odyssey © juganimages
Dreamstime.com

ISBN 978-1-7373499-0-7

Invocation

"Life, to the believer OR the agnostic, is a pretty wonderful affair. I mean wonderful in the sense of true wonder, awful in the sense of awe, stressing the IM in impossible. It is truly a miracle that we are here at all, to sleep, to rise, to down quick breakfasts and run for trains and be on time or late, as Fate decides."

— Ray Bradbury, from the Introduction to *Timeless Stories for Today and Tomorrow*
July 1, 1951

Introduction

And so, the writer writes.

On and on the writer writes, writing of hopes and fears and cliches and ideas, some so mundane he screams with boredom, some so new he laughs with glee, all of them rising unbidden from somewhere behind his eyes, slinking into his heart and streaming down his arm into the fingers of his right hand and onto a page, a page he sometimes doesn't recognize because of the transformation that occurs as the thoughts make their journey to black and white.

"I made this." The child at the end of every *X-Files* episode was so proud and happy to share what s/he made. Likewise, I'm sure, is this little boy with the beer belly with his feet up on the recliner — hoping that what he made is what he meant to say, or failing that, that it means something meaningful enough to enough people that it makes enough of a difference in the world that he may be justifiably proud to say, "I made this."

I made this. It's not really for me to say whether I made something grand or life-changing — although it did change my life to be able to show a finished project to you and declare, yes, indeed, I did make this, and I sincerely hope you're glad I did.

A man in a blue suit bicycles slowly to the finish line — or is it the starting chute? — and nods in my direction.

"So it's you who made this, then? It's something, isn't it? It sure is something. If nothing else, it's the latest project you've completed front to back, and yes, that is something."

Most of this began its life as a blog post. As the collection became more, well, full, I found it separating into three books, one called "The Creative Soul" for better or for worse, a second called "Live Free or Die," and a third full of words of encouragement, perhaps "It's Going to Be All Right" or perhaps "You Can Do This."

And of course, at some point the separate sections were "Rockets," "Bells" and "Poetry," but that was forcing the issue of my subtitle. It's from a 1960s song that Cass Elliott sang, "It's Getting Better" — "Once I believed that when love came to me, it would come with rockets, bells and poetry."

And yes, this is all about love: My love of creating, my love of freedom, my love for encouraging the best in us. My prayer is that you'll find all of that in the pages that follow. Thanks for joining me to see what I made.

Warren Bluhm

June 2021

Book 1
The Creative Soul

FULL

Full

Writing can come in fits and starts, but I am full of words, every day, all day.

At the end of *2001: A Space Odyssey*, astronaut Dave Bowman goes on a bizarre trip through strange lights and images.

At the beginning of the sequel *2010: The Year We Make Contact*, we learn that Bowman's last transmission received on Earth was, "My God, it's full of stars."

My God, I'm full of words.

It's only that I don't always write them down, but when I do ... catharsis.

The dance of the pen across the page is a deer prancing in the snow, kids racing through the grass, a performance car zipping across the flats so fast the videographer struggles to keep the machine in the frame.

When it works, the words flow like water.

When it doesn't, the words drip – drip – drip –

and then stop.

Welcome to my library

Here in the place where the wind chimes peal like church bells in the Lord's steeple,

Here in the place where mythical creatures and legends come to play,

Here in the place where traveling the stars is child's play,

Here in the place where quests and heroes come to dance,

Here in the place where centuries of creative energy are preserved inexpertly but with quiet enthusiasm,

Here in the place of calm before and after the storm,

Here in the place where words play and metaphors gambol in far-flung fields of clover,

Here in the place where crimson and clover make an apt combination,

Here in the place where there's a song to sing and heaven to pay,

Here in the place where tomorrow is a solemn promise and a rousing adventure,

I greet you with joy and whimsy.

I was born near the spring equinox, on the first day of the fourth week of March.

Music has always drawn me in, and so has a good story — and sometimes bad stories — and always wonder stories, superheroes and spaceships and dinosaurs and giants and princesses who slay dragons.

All those dreams are in this place, and so I fold a blanket around my shoulders and open the nearest one. The last thing I want to do is stop dreaming.

There are two chairs here. Sit, and enjoy.

Waiting to be found again

The books wait on the shelves. They came to the shelves, some on impulse, some on purpose, all because they called to me, looking interesting.

Some I bought after a great ebook experience, to preserve the memory to sample again someday. Some are collections of memories (the comic-book compilations and other anthologies). Like the records and the CDs and the DVDs and the iTunes app, they wait for an opportunity to be heard again ... to be found again.

My little (by comparison) library has another purpose: to protect and preserve the past for our future. Each copy of each book is an opportunity for its creator and creation to be found again, to call out to another individual someday. I would say I'm an archivist, but that word suggests some organization to the collection.

Or maybe all archives and museums are a bit disorganized, except for their public displays, with back rooms of boxes and shelves full of the past stored willy-nilly and waiting to be found again.

What art says

"See me," say the books on the shelves. "Feel me. Touch me."

The purpose of a work of art, wrapped up in three two-word sentences.

The creative person says, "I made this. See me. Feel me. Touch me."

(Recalling one brilliant bit of writing by Pete Townshend.)

Why books get written

"I want to write a book."

"I want to leave a mark."

And the people who get serious about the idea write the book, and they leave a mark.

These pages are the mark. They say for now and ever, "This is who I was and what I had to say. This is what I saw and what I think it meant.

"These were my struggles, which may resemble your struggles, and how they affected me and how I tried to overcome them, and I write them down so that you may recognize yourself and find help in overcoming yours."

I suppose you have to have unmitigated ego to believe you have something important to say that might help make life a little easier for the people who happen to bump into your words. Or maybe you just have to care enough to try to help other people.

The words to every song

"I want to live," the soul says with every fiber of its being. "I want to soar. I want to fly. I want to dance. I want to feel. I want to run, I want to sit still and drink all this in, I want to swim, I want to float quietly in the sunlight."

When the soul says, "I want to die," it doesn't really. It's folded into despair so deep until it believes peace can't be found in this life. It knows there is soaring to be done somewhere, and maybe in the next plane of existence, the soul can dance.

But the music is *here*, and the dance is at hand. Listen. Move your feet. Breathe. See that? You're dancing.

The song is everywhere if you just listen. All around you are wind and melody and rhythm, everywhere.

And the words to every song are, "I want to live."

So what's stopping you? Live!

Pulling out the stops

One day I stopped writing poems
when I noticed
poets seldom get rich.

One day I stopped writing songs
because I figured
I'd never be a star.

One day I woke up
and realized
those were silly reasons to stop.

The fine art of riding the torrent

Why do the young (supposedly) write the most amazing songs? The Beatles were in their 20s. I know, not so, not so — some of the great works were by mature authors — but maybe foolish youth doesn't know better and unleashes work that hasn't been tinkered and edited to death.

After that first burst of success, they begin to think, "I am a recognized whatever now, and so I am obligated to produce works of genius," as opposed to "I am flowing with the universe and I must share what I experience, I am the conduit not the genius creator, come see and hear what I see and hear."

As soon as the acclaim comes, the pressure is on. "What will you do next" as if that wasn't enough, as if "you" did it. And you start to seek out the inspiration instead of watching and listening.

Yes, there is a flow to be tapped and there is a Great Architect willing to share the vision, and we are creators made in the Architect's image and so the act of creating is built into our genes, but in the trying too hard to craft we can lose sight of the spark — just as these sentences are crawling more slowly out of the pen than they were a couple of minutes ago.

Sometimes, when I get out of my own way, here come the words in a torrent, and as soon as I become conscious of the flow — "Look, mom, it's a torrent!" — it starts to slip away.

Oh, take me away, mad genius, let me swim and swim in the torrent, sharing what I see and hear bursting from my chest like some generous alien critter — not a parasite like in the movie that uses my body and casts it aside, rather a creation-maker who fills my heart and makes it give — an I-don't-know-what that sends my hands flying across the page, and I look back and don't quite remember where it all came from.

Imagine an aging Paul McCartney who never wrote his little masterpiece, sitting down to write and coming up with, "Yesterday all my troubles seemed so far away," and looking at the phrase and thinking, "No, no, no, that's kind of bogus, I can do better than that ..."

It's a trick, letting the universe talk and not judging what you've got until later, and maybe the young are better at it because they haven't learned the unfine art of second guesses. Ray Bradbury said, "Don't think," and I think he was on to something. In thinking comes editing, and from editing comes a trickle instead of a torrent, with only what seems best in the moment coming out.

Somewhere in the torrent will be the real gem, and you must let the river run through you, the wild river untamed and roaring along with all of it, not just the trickle, and then come back and say "Some force possessed me," not "Oh look, see what I contrived to create this morning."

And that is what comes of not thinking.

We are the writers

We write our pain. We write our joy.

We write our anger. We write our fear.

We write our peace. We write our love.

Oh, how we write our love.

We write to think. We write to feel.

We write to understand. We write to comprehend.

We write to figure it out and we write to be nonsensical.

And oh, how we write our love.

We write to remember. We write to forget.

We write to dream. We write our nightmares.

We write to predict. We write to preserve.

In other words, we write.

In these exact words, we write.

We write until there are too many words to read,

until there are not enough, until they're just so.

We write for all the right reasons.

We write for all the wrong reasons.

We write to get it right. We write to steer you wrong.

We write and write and write and write and write

As if we were stuck in Casablanca

With nothing to do but wait and wait and wait

and as long as we were waiting so long

we may as well write.

From ether to planet

Here are the heroes of time immemorial
Locked in the struggle that lasts for all time;
Here are the questions and some of the answers
Waiting for someone to call them by name,
Here in the vault tucked away in Elysian,
Here in the hearts of the beings named poets,
Not asking, but asking, and serving as pages
To carry the message from on beyond here.
Here are they all, all the words and the music,
Raging and loving and seeking and found
Until they come pouring and flowing on pages
To find immortality or flash in the pan.
Alone and forgotten, familiar and beloved,
The words sing in silence till spoken aloud.
The words sing in silence till spoken aloud.

The Creative Soul

A poem is a dance of rhythm and words;
The melody's added to make it a song.
Is it less of a song if you hold back the tune?
I guess that's the question the rappers have answered
For better or worse, and the talking plods on.

Rhythm — then words — or melody first;
Does the dancing come first, or was it the last?
Capture the wind and the rustling of branches,
Capture the moanings of joy and of sorrow,
Add then the beat and now you are singing
What we call a song, at its deepest a sob.

Am I writing one poem or a series of short ones?
It's not mine to question while all the words flow.
Just lay down what's coming from ether to planet
And worry details when the moment has passed.
Yes, it's a communion of ghosts and of spirits;
I cannot explain where it's all coming from.
I'm just the receiver of what's pouring forward,
I'm just a poor poet encased in a trance
That clears away quickly as soon as I'm conscious
And my unconscious subconscious drives me away —

FULL

"Get out of here, man, if you don't want to play!

I'll find some poor soul who is ready for me,

More ready than your questions allow you to be!"

... And the wind chimes dance in the breeze ...

I do love letting the words fly —

Here in the morning, here in this chair,

Coffee cup on my belly, the muse in the air,

Such as she is, trying hard with this sod —

Any transcription issues are on me, not on her.

Sometimes the music is lost in translation,

But sometimes the song saunters through clear as air.

Books like grenades

What is more dangerous than a room full of books? Books, stacked in pules and lined in rows, each with a purpose and a reason, waiting to be lifted up and hurled like a grenade into what once was someone's unconscious subconscious. Books, dragging her kicking and screaming into consciousness.

Beware the book: It will reach from one mind into another and detonate previously unknown insights and concepts.

"Weaponizing books?" he sniffed. "Child's play. You can weaponize anything if you put your mind to it. Give me a fluffy puppy and I'll soften a million of you up for the kill – although I don't need to kill you, I just need you to go away and leave me to my evil games. Did I say evil? My heavens. No one is intentionally evil; we all are the heroes of our own internal stories, aren't we?"

The gleam in his eye was unmistakable: Cold and evil.

A cluttered mind journals in cluttered room

(Stares at the blank page, then at the bitter cold view out the window — sunny, but treacherous — then up at the clock and at the Julia Cameron book left next to the other armchair instead of back up on the shelf where it belongs.)

What is the problem with having "a place for everything and everything in its place"? Why do I just leave everything where I left it, lost and disheveled in a place not its own? How will I ever find it there? Rolling my eyes at myself asking, "Now where did I put that?" or stumbling over it in the dark or forgetting it even exists until one day, sorting through a pile, I see it and think, "OMG, I was supposed to do something with this," or "OMG, now I remember what I meant to do before Christmas," or "THAT was it."

(Sees the fedora lying on top of a pile of 1990s-era Writer's Digest magazines, and the cardboard lid for a cardboard box long ago recycled, and the HDMI cables from the TV units disconnected two weeks ago.)

They say, "Let sleeping dogs lie," but I have so much debris on the floor in places where a dog might want to lay down and have a nap, so they can't. Am I genetically predisposed to live in a pig sty, or is that just something frustrated mothers say?

I have a vision for this room, and I never get around to finishing it. There's the microphone and the mixing board and the guitars on the wall and the turntable next to everything, and the computers ready to convert the sounds into something to share — or ready to accept the words that will become books one day.

(Gets up to let a dog in and picks up the Julia Cameron book before sitting down, then sets the book next to the chair and picks the journal back up.)

If I start reading, am I avoiding my writing? Am I reading and writing when I ought to be logging into the day job? Or will the reading and the writing make me better at all of this — or at least end up decluttering one of the cluttered areas in this room? How does a 10-by-10 room get so cluttered in the first place? And if everything were to be in its place, would I remember where all those places are?

(Gets up to retrieve a figurine the cat just knocked down the stairs. It's a childlike figure of Joseph, separated from Mary and Jesus by a playful feline. Good thing the stairs are carpeted.)

Yes, we still have our little artificial Christmas tree up on its shelf and the seasonal decorations around it. Do you know how comforting it is, with the outside temperature hovering around zero Fahrenheit and the metaphorical chill settled around the land, to be reminded of a time when we celebrated the birth of a man of peace, who tried to revolutionize the way we treat one another? When all is said and done about him, the things I remember most are that he said to love our neighbors — and everyone is our neighbor — and not to worry. Who of us by worrying can add a day to our lifetimes? OK, maybe worrying can spur action that saves a day, but he just meant there are better ways to spend a day than worrying to death — and the "Love one another" part was the more important thing anyway.

(Uncrosses a leg and crosses the other one. Changes the ink refill on his favorite pen. Pets the dog that just stuck her nose on the chair's arm.) (It's the other dog — is it her turn to go out, or does she just want to keep me company?)

We never know exactly what the right thing to do is — and so we keep doing what we were doing until a better idea or more urgent need presents itself. One important thing is to act on the better idea before it devolves into a more urgent need.

A brief lesson in writing and self-forgiveness

"Hello. My name is x and my mind wanders."

"Hi, x," intoned the others in the group.

"I've been sitting here for 20 minutes, and my head has been all over the place. I glanced at my phone until I realized what I was doing. I read some back pages of my journal, I sipped coffee, I added to the to-do list for today, and what I didn't do until a few moments ago was write. It's funny, because I call myself a writer. On the other hand, I recently discovered that preparing my mind to write is part of the writing process, but if all that fussing was prep, then I have prepared for 20 minutes during a period when I had 25 minutes total to write something."

"Still," one of the others said, "you did write something. So stop beating on yourself."

When the drought broke

"You only fail if you stop writing."

My mentor's gentle eyes bore into my soul. He knew that I'd written every day for six days, just as I'd planned, and on the second 15 days I'd rested.

"You only fail if you stop writing," he said.

"I know, I know. You're right. I failed," I said.

"So write."

"I will," I said.

"You only fail if you stop writing," he said. "'I will' is not 'I am.'"

"I know."

"You only fail if you stop writing," he said. " 'I know' is not 'I am.'"

I took a deep breath.

And wrote:

"In a land far away there was a lone rider. What he was riding is a little hard to explain if you've never been to that far

*away land. It was soft like a pampered dog but big like a horse, but
with a smushier face than a horse or a dog, but not so smushy that
it was a human or an ape. So: A larger snout than ours but shorter
than theirs. But big enough to ride comfortably and big enough that
it didn't mind so much being ridden.*

*"I suspect, though, that you don't want to know about the
animal so much as the lone rider. Why was he alone? Where was
he going? Where was he coming from? And what is the dark secret
that complicated his life to the point where he was making this
journey alone?"*

"That's better," my mentor smiled. "Go on."

*"The dust on the rider's clothing and the weary gait of the
animal told us they had been riding for a very long time — hours,
or even days. The animal couldn't or wouldn't talk, and the rider
had nothing to say. The miles went by slowly in silence. A barely
noticeable path through a large flat plain, the sun bearing down on
amber waves. Not a desert, but not a lush land or a wooded plain
by any stretch. And still silence everywhere."*

"I see what you did there," my mentor said. "'Still
silence ...'"

"Thank you."

"You only fail if you stop writing."

"But it's time for breakfast."

"And you have written. It's so easy, isn't it?"

"Only when I take the time."

"So ..."

"I'll take the time."

"Good lad. Go eat."

The value of being real

"People want their wisdom in short bursts."

"People want their stories long and complicated."

People — people — people — what do YOU want? How do the wisdom generators and storytellers reach YOU?

That's the puzzle, and that's the solution: You are not "people." You are person. You have a name. You might enjoy the cookie made with a cookie cutter, created to fit "the market," and you might not.

How do I reach you? By giving the universe what I would want to see— providing the most authentic version of me that I can muster — and hoping you find it.

It's not quite as random as that, but it's close. And being The Real Me is my best shot at reaching The Real You.

Gladness is Infectious

Gladness is infectious

But so can be despair

So seek out reasons

to be glad

mon frère

When the spigot turns

I can't just turn the spigot and the words come pouring out into rockets, bells and poetry. I have to sit in an easy chair and THEN turn the spigot.

I have to pick up a pen or turn on the computer and imagine a girl whose mother was an explorer of time and space and dimensions. I have to look out the window and write down what I see. I have to listen to music and feel what I feel and then tell you. I have to read a book about living on Prince Edward Island during a terrible war overseas and process what that was like. I have to jump at the sound of a bird being surprised that the open space into my well-lit room is a barrier he couldn't see — and hope he wasn't dashing so fast to get into this space that he's crumpled and forever gone below. (He wasn't.)

In short, I have to live and, living, write the life into words.

Everything I see and hear and feel and smell and taste is something to write about. It all collects inside, welling up in the well, until I sit down and turn the spigot.

And so, on a morning when I'm not sure what to write, I just start the fingers to forming words and see what they tell me.

Just. Show. Up.

It was one of those scattered mornings where day-job deadlines loomed and my mind rebelled against the idea of staying in one place and doing The Work first — you know, The Work, not the stuff that brings home the bacon but the other stuff, the stories and the blog posts and the magical music of words — the fun.

I have been trying to take The Work as seriously as I've always taken the day job, and so I sat, a little tense and unfocused but determined to robot my way through the morning writing routine if I had to. In the back of my mind, I kept hearing all the clocks in the house tick and thinking about photographs I had to process and news stories I had to write and edit, even though I had set this special sacred time aside to write things like, I don't know, soaring over the bay chasing a pelican to ask how the view is up here and if you ever grow weary of bringing home the carp or the perch or whatever it is that pelicans dine on.

FULL

It was always "Maybe if I buckle down and get the work-work done, then I'll have time for the fun stuff later," but it always became later later later, and then the day was over and the fun stuff didn't happen, so I committed to sitting down to attempt to do The Work now, not later, but instead I'm moping instead of doing fun stuff —

And then, just like that, my fingers raced across the page and gave me some insight into the main adversary in the novel I'm writing, more than a page of wild fantastic spunk. For a few minutes the day job vanished and I was inside the mind of a Venusian prince mansplaining his evil sister's motivations.

Wait, what?

How did that happen?

Pay attention here, friends: I wrote a handful of paragraphs about how distracted I was because I had so much work to do and I didn't really have time to do any of the creative stuff I wanted to do ...

And then, BAM! For a few precious moments I created something cool, something I can fold into the Big Project I'm Working On When I Can.

But see what I did there?

I wrote! I didn't think I had time, I kept thinking about all the other stuff I had to do, and the first few things I wrote were about woe-is-me-I-wish-I-had-time-to-concentrate.

But I wrote! I didn't think, "Crap, I don't have time for this today," and blow it off. I sat down and wrote, and it was junk and whining and worthless until it wasn't, until I was writing a page about why the villain in my story is so villainous and how she learned to mistreat people the way she does, and oh my goodness I didn't have time for this but I forced myself to take a little time anyway and a little corner of my novel suddenly blossomed.

Because I wrote. I had less than 15 minutes to spare, and I couldn't concentrate, but I sat down to write. And that's the moral of the story.

They say that 90 percent of art is just showing up. I got an illustration of that basic fact right there. Wow, says I. Just wow.

You do art, right? That's what brought you here. I'm here to tell you because I just relearned it: Even if you have only a couple of minutes to spare, sit down and spare those minutes. Your art will honor your commitment and gift you.

FULL

Because I refused to skip my morning writing session that morning, my evil princess is that much eviler. (And by the way, I made my day-job deadlines. Bonus.)

Honor your art. Practice your art. Seize your minutes. Just show up and do your art.

Trusting in the possibilities

The possibilities are endless.

I look around my room and part of me is overwhelmed. How does it always get this messy? I'm like a kid who doesn't know to put away his toys, leaving a pile of stuff everywhere I turn.

It's like that when I sit down to write some mornings. What could I possibly write? It's not: "I got nothing." No, it's: "So many choices!" How do you pick just one toy?

What wonder have I assembled within a couple of steps and an easy reach. Here are books collecting the first 50 editions of Fantastic Four, the first 40 editions of Spider-Man, similar collections of Batman and Captain Marvel and Zot. Not far away are *A Treasury of Sherlock Holmes*, a collection of Henry Wadsworth Longfellow poetry, all of Edgar Rice Burroughs' John Carter stories — right here at my elbow is the Emily Dickinson paperback I pulled off the shelf a couple of weeks ago, and Carole King is singing "Smackwater Jack" from the turntable.

Is there a more perfect album of songs than *Tapestry*? OK, *Blue* and *Judee Sill* are also within reach, so I can think of plenty of contenders just in my own collection. But still ... "When my soul was in the lost and found, you came along to claim it ..."

The robin eggs under our back deck have hatched, and mama is tending what were little fluffballs not long ago but this morning look, amazingly, like little robins.

And what a few weeks ago was a white landscape is now awash with green. It has always been my favorite color, green, speaking as it does of life and warmth and growth.

Sometimes I sit in my chair, pen posed expectantly over the page, and my fingers just hover. It's not that I don't know what to write. It's that the possibilities are endless.

At those moments I have a choice to be frustrated, or I can remember the story of a friend who needed to start work on a promotional video for his nonprofit, but so many things called for his attention, he didn't know where to begin.

"Just get started," smiled the renowned actor who had agreed to appear in his video. "The rest will take care of itself."

And so I send my fingers across the page — or the keyboard as I'm doing now — and see what happens. It's not magic, it's just trusting in the possibilities.

I suppose I should pick up some of this mess. What would company think? If I keel over unexpectedly today, how rude of me to leave this for someone else to pick up. It's like wearing dirty underwear to the emergency room.

Even more important, though, there may be something miraculous waiting to be rediscovered. How cool is that?

Righting

Is something bothering you? Start writing.

Something's wrong. You're not sure what it is but you're uneasy — or you know exactly what's wrong and you're seething or brokenhearted or just upset. Start writing.

Don't worry about what to write. Write about what's wrong — that's easy, it's the main thing on your mind. Write why it's upsetting you and what in the world you're going to do about it — fix it, walk away, whatever — go through the options if you're not sure.

After a while something amazing will happen. As you see the problem unfold — literally — you'll start to see solutions and options and all the other things a person does to deal with problems. And you'll feel better because writing it down gave you more control over the situation, or at least more understanding.

"Writing 'rights' things," Julia Cameron wrote. Want to see how that works? Start writing.

Do

Keep moving.

Keep creating.

Do.

Forget the "or do not."

Just do.

There is no "or."

Yes, there is no "try."

But once committed,

there is no choice.

Your dreams and wishes can come true

"A dream does not work unless you do," said the sign. It's true.

"I can only write when the inspiration strikes," said the author. "Fortunately it strikes at precisely 9 a.m. every day."

"God helps those who help themselves" may not be a biblical quote, but it makes a good point. "A person makes his own luck through hard work."

You can wish on as many stars as you like, but the key to making your dreams come true is to make your dreams come true. Make. Your. Dreams. Come True.

Oh, wishing is not a bad thing. The power of "I wish" is that the words that follow define what you want. But simply wishing doesn't make it happen.

Set your mind. Do the work. And then the dreams start coming true.

It isn't enough to know who and what you want to be – you need to get down to the business of becoming. You need to earn the rest at the end of the day.

You have to intentionally dive in and roll up sleeves and grab the tools and do the work. And work is not a flurry of activity and movement and no purpose; you have to know the why and the when and the where.

Use all your time

Wow, that was something you just created — meme worthy at least, maybe something timeless.

What else you got?

It's easy to look at what you've just written and say, "There! Done! Mission accomplished!" and go back to life. But there are still hours in the day, or at least minutes in the creative time you carved out.

What else you got?

The Beatles had a few minutes left in the studio time they'd purchased to record an album. So they did a couple of takes of "Twist and Shout," which is a legendary recording. Or am I mixing that story up with the story of Barry McGuire and "Eve of Destruction"?

The point is, if you strike genius midway through and still have time left, keep going. You still have gas in the tank, so keep burning it. Don't let the knowledge of one bit of wonderfulness sit fat and sassy in your ego while another bit goes sailing past undiscovered.

If you said, "I have a half-hour to create something cool" and you have something cool in eight minutes, don't rest on your laurels for 22 more minutes. Maybe you're on a roll and something cooler is about to emerge. Maybe your story will be "that day I created three of my most beloved pieces in a half-hour."

You already know you've got "that day I created something amazing in eight minutes," so why not? Finish the session. Spend your allotted time. Give all you've got in the time that's left. You might change the world again, and there's your story.

Your mission,
should you decide to accept

Give yourself permission.

Sing a song. Play a musical instrument.

Write a poem. Paint a painting. Create a pot.

Draw what you see, either in front of your nose or in your head.

Move your hands. Move your body.

Make something that didn't exist until your hands started playing.

Create. Make. Build. You are human. That's what humans do.

It all begins when you
Give yourself permission.

Just write

It doesn't have to be a poem.
It doesn't have to be a song.
It doesn't have to be anything,
not yet — just write.

Let loose the hounds of more!
Pour the words onto the page
in quantity, searching for quality,
diamonds in the rough — no, not even that,
just send the words — no, not even,
just pull the words from the ether
and thank the Muse,

just thank the Muse,
and run back to the well
        for more

Book 2
Live Free Or Die

FULL

That's enough

Enough!

Enough shouting in anger and indignation and oh so outrage. Enough, sez I.

Enough woe is me I wish life were easier.

Enough crying how dark it is out there.

Enough, enough, enough.

Yep, we've all heard enough angry partisans to last us a lifetime. I've heard enough indignant mutterings to know you're indignant. I've heard enough outrage to understand some people would rather be perpetually outraged. Enough crying in the dark to see some people are more comfortable in the dark than doing something to turn on a light.

It's too tired and draining to be angry and outraged all the time.

I'm going to break out in pursuit of peaceful voices, acceptance, understanding, and laughing. Definitely more laughing needed around here.

Freedom and the things of state

I try to send optimism and hope into the world, or at least a bit of sanity. Days come and go when I despair over the state of things, of course, because the state of things grows more dire as the things of state gain more and more power.

But the space between my ears is as free as ever, fragile though that space may be, and it will be ever so while this trusty heart is pumping away.

And as long as free women and men walk the planet, it's going to be all right. And since freedom is endowed on every living soul from birth, it will be ever so.

Who knows how long I'll be able to write and speak my mind? Answer: As long as my mind is able. The question is more "Who knows how long I'll be *permitted* to write and speak my mind freely?" and those days seem to be growing shorter.

But spring will be here in two months, and the days are literally growing longer. There are seasons of freedom and tyranny just as there are spring, summer, fall, and winter, and the time will come when the free will marvel at how much power was given to the censors and other bullies of our time.

Some wish to resolve our differences with guns and bombs and screams and violence, but those inevitably lead to a response of more guns and bombs and screams and violence. A gentle word turns away wrath — eventually. Reason is superior to brute force, although reasonable people need to bear many scars before they succeed. Peace through reason has a longer shelf life than peace through war, however. More people seek the words of the peacekeepers — Gandhi, MLK, Thoreau — than those of the assassins.

Sometimes I forget and join the chorus of anger, because I too am human — or I am too human. On the days when I turn from anger and seek peace, I find freedom.

Nothing's the matter

"What's the matter?" Red asked when she made a 4 a.m. pit stop and saw me sitting in my office writing in my journal.

"Nothing's the matter," I said. "I just couldn't get back to sleep."

And it was true. Yes, I'd given up trying to go back to la-la land after 15-20 minutes of my mind bouncing around about things that needed to be done that day, preparing for a coming snowstorm, clipping dog nails, cleaning my messy office, getting back to practicing guitar, reading Discworld books, writing Jeep Thompson books, writing blog posts, marketing my books, listening to the wind chimes trying to fade back to sleep, thinking about day-job issues, streaming consciousness ...

But by the time Red asked what the matter was, it didn't matter, and I was just journaling and exploring ...

I was finding the dance in the chaos.

I was finding the rhythm in the maelstrom.

I was hearing the melody in those wind chimes.

Nothing's the matter. We spend too much time looking for The Matter and not enough time enjoying the perfection, too much time building cases against one another and not enough time dancing. Do you remember how to dance?

We spend so much time contemplating what ails us and not-so-much time enjoying our health.

There comes a time in every song when the words must pause and let the melody sing.

We keep looking for problems when the joy of living is right in front of us.

merry-go-round

The war ended, and peace was at hand.
The people celebrated by making babies, a veritable boom of
babies.
But the old men had other ideas
and they conjured new wars.

And one day the baby boom grew to old men
and started new wars of their own.

Who will be the first
to cry "peace"?

Heed the quiet

Take a deep breath and listen for peace,
and you will find it.

The world calls us to chaos,
but if we pause to listen,
there is that still small voice
— hear it?

Turn from the chaos and listen.

That moment you realize you're being lied to

(with grateful thanks to George Orwell, H.L. Mencken, Dr. Seuss and Joss Whedon)

Winston Smith sat in a corner where he was pretty sure the telescreen couldn't see him, and he wrote in a journal. He questioned whether the vision of reality that came from state-controlled media was true. The more he thought and the words flowed from his mind and fingers, the angrier and more frustrated he felt, until he realized he was writing over and over, DOWN WITH BIG BROTHER. DOWN WITH BIG BROTHER.

Are human beings brutish and violent at their core? Is there nothing, when all veneer is stripped away, except violence and hatred? That is what they would have us believe – or perhaps: That is what they believe, and so they appeal to our hatred and the dark corner of our souls that most of us keep in check but some of us exercise in the most horrifying ways.

Some of these manipulators express themselves with blunt force trauma – name calling and insults and straightforward hate. Others are more subtle – barely – separating us into intellectual camps and cubby holes by race and creed and gender and religion and sexual preferences until the categorization of individuals into groups creates a list longer than your arm, and then claiming to be champions of each cubby hole. But oh, those who object to the categorization of individuals, a special hatred is reserved for those people.

As H.L. Mencken said, the whole aim of practical politics is to keep the populace alarmed (and therefore more willing to turn to the practical politician to be led to safety) through an endless series of imaginary hobgoblins.

Imaginary. Hobgoblins. The threat of the other.

The practical politician says, "I will save you. I will rescue you from the other. Trust me to lead you to safety. Put your safety and security in my hands and I will give you peace. Let me attach this leash to your neck to better guide you. Let me explain the rules you must follow to keep your behavior and your property in line. Do you trust me? Give me your life."

FULL

But here in the quiet, away from the clamoring of the politicians, no thuggishness and violence ooze from our core – just relief and an awe of the miracle that is life. Our neighbor is an individual, not a group member, and he/she is working to make a better life, to survive, to feed her family, just like anyone else. I don't know and I don't care if he prefers his toast butter side up or butter side down. I have no need to beat him; I just want to go my way. (Dr. Seuss and Joss Whedon references back to back. Whoa.)

I am weary of being told my neighbor is – or I am – the cause of all the turmoil in the world. I am weary of being told that my neighbor – or I – is a threat to the rest of us. I am weary of being told that my neighbor is – or I am – a hobgoblin. I know my neighbor, and I know myself. I see no hobgoblins, only angry and grasping demagogues pointing to imaginary hobgoblins in every direction. I know that I am not the hobgoblin they say I am – and if they are wrong about me, they are probably wrong about my neighbor.

Political conventions and campaigns are Orwell's Hate Minute on steroids. Perhaps if there are true hobgoblins, they are the ones who organize these hate fests. We need no politicians to lead us to safety from exaggerated or nonexistent threats, and certainly not by turning our power and our freedom over to them.

They are – and listen to me falling into the same rhetorical trap. "They." "Us." "Them."

Assailed by hobgoblins, we organize into camps, and when we run out of hobgoblins, we present another camp as the new hobgoblin – but all of it is a figment of our imaginations.

Both major parties engage in this. Both major parties have elevated warriors who extol the dangers of imaginary hobgoblins – no hobgoblin more dangerous than the other party's warrior.

Here's the bottom line: They both want you delirious with fear and hate. Don't give them that pleasure. And above all, don't turn your freedom over to them. Down with Big Brother.

People want peace

There it was, in the middle of a writing exercise where the mentor said "number a page from 1 to 25 and write 25 sentences as fast as you can, beginning with the words "I wish ..."

In the middle of things like "I wish I exercised more" and "I wish I would finish my novels" and such, there it was:

I wish people didn't hate so much.

It seems we are so quick to anger, so quick to take offense, so quick to find fault and even evil in other people, so quick to hate.

So here is my plea for peace, here in the quiet of Monday morning when the only sounds are the clocks ticking, the drip of the coffee maker, the refrigerator's humming, a cat's hungry grumble, and oh, I guess I'm breathing softly.

Here, Monday morning, before any of us have a chance to lose our tempers, I'm just asking you to remember:

People want peace.

Don't they?

You will find what you seek

If this be the new Dark Age, greet it with sunshine.

If this is the time of anger and hate, greet it with peace and love.

If this is the time of "give me what I deserve," be generous.

Resentment is a dime a dozen; gratitude is precious and eternal.

Seek out reasons to be glad about this life, and you will find them.

Seek out reasons to be bitter and entitled, and you will find those, too.

I can tell you life is sweeter when you search for the light in the darkness, not the other way around.

All things lead to hope

There it is again. Hear it? A spark of life, and where life is, there is hope.

The ruins of yesterday can be rebuilt. The harsh edges may be smoothed over. The debris and the wreckage can be cleared away and replaced by new, glistening structures built on a foundation of love and peace.

The pessimist will say nothing good lasts forever, but neither does anything evil. All things must pass, which makes the good things more precious and the bad things more bearable.

At the start, today is a blank sheet, an open space to be filled. And let it be filled with wonder, and joy, and perhaps a bit of whimsy, and surely with a hope for an even better tomorrow.

Let the words of my mouth and the meditation in my heart be on these things, the fruits of the Spirit, the best of our angels, the machinery of joy.

Holding these truths

Your happiness is independent of Washington.

You do understand that, right?

All the brouhaha and machinations and puffery and, yes, silliness, it has nothing to do with your everyday life. Even the terrible events of this past week didn't interrupt what you were doing.

That's what it means to be free.

And please make no mistake:

You're free. Nothing is stopping you.

Go! Flex those arms and legs and start walking — run if you wish.

It's your decision to walk, run, crawl, growl, or sit and wait. The choices are all yours.

You have to own the results, of course — that's how life works in a free society — but don't let that thought stop you, either.

Yeah: It's those thoughts that you let stop you that really hurt.

It all comes back to this thought: We hold these truths to be self-evident, that all folks are created equal with certain rights that can't be taken away, including the right to life, liberty, and the pursuit of happiness.

Washington didn't give you these rights, and Washington can't take them away, no matter how much it may try. You were born with them.

So go ahead. Get out there and pursue happiness.

How can I help you

Not gonna win the lottery ...
Not gonna have a ship that comes in outta nowhere ...
No rich uncles to bail me out ...
No precious gems buried under my backyard ...
I guess I'm going to have to earn my keep ...
same as millions who've gone before:
Do some good for other folks, and
Create something they can value or use.

To be of worth: The wise man said you can have
anything you want in this life, if you'll just help enough
other people get what they want. It's as simple, and as
complicated as all that.

"What value can I add to the world today?" Not "What
can I sell someone?"

They are different ways of saying the same thing with a
different focus: How can I help you? What can I sell you?
What can we give each other? What can we share?

How can I help you? — such a common question, and yet, sincerely intended, it's the foundation of all peace and prosperity.

Peace and prosperity? Of course, because people who have what they need are not interested in disrupting lives, theirs or anybody else's. People who have what they want are, by definition, prosperous.

Creating value for one's neighbors — and defining everyone as our neighbors — is the road to peace.

Seizing value without a fair exchange? That's how wars begin.

A signal to burst the chains

Not long ago I was browsing through a book called *The Essential Thomas Jefferson*, a collection that – like all "Essential" albums – includes his greatest hits and a rich selection of deep cuts. The following is excerpted from the final entry in the book, a letter to Roger C. Weightman written June 24, 1826, two weeks before Jefferson died.

The letter leaves the old man feeling as if his mission was fulfilled and with the hope that what he and his fellows had accomplished 50 years earlier would continue to serve as a beacon to humanity.

The old way of thinking – that some people are born to rule the rest of us – continues to plague the world. Too many in our nation and around the world believe government exists to control the lives of the mass of humanity that doesn't know any better. But to those who understand each of us was indeed born with certain, unalienable rights, the actions Jefferson and his colleagues took in July 1776 do still shine in history.

And so, writing of American independence and that historic day:

May it be to the world, what I believe it will be (to some parts sooner, to others later, but finally to all) – the signal of arousing men to burst the chains under which monkish ignorance and superstition has persuaded them to bind themselves, and to assume the blessings and security of self-government. That form which we have substituted restores the free right to the unbounded exercise of reason and freedom of opinion. All eyes are opened, or opening, to the rights of man. The general spread of the light of science has already laid open to every view the palpable truth that the mass of mankind has not been born with saddles on their backs, nor a favored few booted and spurred, ready to ride them legitimately, by the grace of God. These are grounds of hope for others. For ourselves, let the annual return of this day forever refresh our recollections of these rights, and an undiminished devotion to them.

Free people seek the light, always

I wish I could remember where I saw it, and I wish I had written it down, or saved it, or printed it out, but I don't and I didn't, so ...

You'll just have to take my word for it. (You do remember when a person's word was his/her bond, right?)

Some time back I read about a historian who had tracked civilization's ups and downs in waves, and this person predicted that the next great downward wave, a downturn bordering on dark ages, would begin in 2020.

I think about that article lately.

But it's in my nature to seek the light.

Not long ago I wrote about how glad I am to live in a land where people drafted a Bill of Rights to restrict bad people from doing bad things, tyrannical things, to everyday people. Even though they still do bad things, tyrannical things, at least there's a standard against which those things can be judged bad.

When the age looks very dark, that's a very dim light to hang my hat on, I know. Barely a candle's flicker on a breezy day.

Many of my favorite works of fiction are dystopian: *Nineteen Eighty-Four*, of course, and *Animal Farm*, and the 1960s TV show *The Prisoner* with its iconic shout of defiance: "I am not a number, I am a free man!"

Notice that: Held captive in a Village where faceless rulers insist that everyone think and act the same, where contrary thought is punished and no one may leave, this person cries, "I am a free man!"

And he is.

And, as darkness appears to be falling, and bad people are attempting to shepherd everyone into sheepish little villages and silence everyone who doesn't think or act correctly, that flicker refuses to be extinguished.

We are free. Many don't quite understand, but that's The Thing about freedom: We are "endowed at birth" with it, so it's always ours to exercise or surrender.

Bullies love to try forcing free people to surrender, but we keep reading and collecting the banned books, gathering in groups or retreating in solitary to speak and write what we please, creating great art and great businesses that free the mind, body and soul.

The response to tyranny's violence is not more violence, because that plays into the bully's hands. The bully can only tear down; the free person builds, always. No, the response is simply to be free. The tyrant needs your permission to take your freedom, and you needn't give it.

If a new dark age is starting, then we protect the light. Every warming campfire begins with a flicker.

Emerging from Dystopia

An article making the rounds the other day noted that Ray Bradbury predicted all this, writing in his dystopian classic *Fahrenheit 451*, that people would demand tyranny and censorship, that it would not be forced upon us but enforced by popular demand. Yes, Bradbury's book does contain that bleakness.

But —

But *Fahrenheit 451* ends with hope, with Granger talking about a silly damn bird called a Phoenix that burned itself up every few hundred years and then got himself born all over again, adding that we're the same but we've got one thing the Phoenix didn't have: the ability to remember all the silly damn things we've done, and as long as we know that and remember, some day we'll stop making the goddam funeral pyres and jumping in the middle of them.

"And some day we'll remember so much that we'll build the biggest goddam steamshovel in history and dig the biggest grave of all time and shove war in and cover it up. Come on now, we're going to go build a mirror-factory first and put out nothing but mirrors for the next year and take a long look in them."

Every generation has people who remember and preserve the lessons and whisper encouragement to the peacemakers. Every generation we gain a few more who remember, and oh so quietly the biggest goddam steamshovel in history is being assembled, and someday someone is going to stop before he throws a punch or a Molotov cocktail or burns a book, and he'll say to himself, "How stupid is this?"

Sometime after the end of *Fahrenheit 451*, someone found an old printing press and dusted it off and oiled it up and started making books, a little at a time, and people taught each other how to read them and write them and start to understand each other again.

That's the difference between this novel and the other great dystopian works — *Nineteen Eighty-four and Brave New World* have bleak endings, the individual crushed by Big Brother and the gaping foolishness of society, but *Fahrenheit 451* ends with hope, because Bradbury saw the potential in the heart of humanity. He looked up and saw the stars.

o o o o o

And what else will people remember?

That all are created equal, endowed by their Creator with certain, unalienable rights, including the right to life, the right to liberty, and the right to pursue happiness. "Endowed by their Creator," not by the bosses, rights that were ours from the moment of creation, rights we have held since birth, and let no tyrant try to take them away. He or she may send armies to lock you down, but they cannot crush your rights without your permission.

In dystopia, no one talks about freedom. But some remember. They hold the memory delicately like a flower that might be crushed, but freedom is not so fragile. Freedom is baked into our DNA and forged into our souls. Our instinct to be free is slapped and shoved and slashed and burned, but it is impervious to all.

"They may take our lives, but they will never take our freedom." It's a line in a movie, spoken by a character who lived and died 700 years ago. In another film a man is chained for calling out liars among their wannabe rulers, and he rattles the handcuff and declares, "I am the only free man on this train."

FULL

In the stories, those men died, but we remember them, and we remember what they said.

o o o o o

There was an empire and an emperor, and neither could see faces; they only saw the people, and they treated the people as if they were their children, and they taught the people to serve the emperor and the empire, but they never saw the faces, they only saw the mass, and they didn't see that inside that mass were infinite numbers of faces, and many were hurting, and many suffered.

But one day, a person stood up and said, "I have an idea." And another called back, "I've had that idea, too." And others said, "Yes, and here's another idea." And all of them had faces. That was how it began, you see: That was how people began to stop thinking of themselves as "the masses" and began to see each other.

They realized that there was no single, amorphous mass, only a great number of individuals with the ability to work together in harmony, each of them so powerful that a proverb said, "When an old person dies, a library burns to the ground." When they understood that the true power resides inside each individual, the false and manufactured power of the empire began to fade, until it came to pass that everyone understood the emperor was simply another individual, no greater or lesser than any other of us.

Darkness descends, and night may last a very long time, but some of us remember and whisper about the light and the promise and the face of hope. That may not be much, but some day it will be enough.

o o o o o

Post-apocalyptic literature assumes that a cataclysm of some kind is the inevitable climax to dystopia — but catastrophe is always avoidable, until it isn't. A series of choices makes the situation worse and worse until Big Brother micromanages lives (*Nineteen Eighty-Four*) or the populace lives in a drugged stupor (*Brave New World*) or people demand books be banned or even burned (*Fahrenheit 451*), or all of the above (2020).

But it doesn't have to end with scorched earth, until, of course, the landscape is scorched. At any time before that, the disaster can be avoided.

In *Fahrenheit 451*, the earth is scorched, but there's a sense that we will rebuild. This is scant consolation to those who must do the work of rebuilding, of moving from scorched earth to Eden, but scant consolation is better than inconsolable.

The challenge always is finding a way to avoid the cataclysm, to stop short of Ragnarok and move straight to Eden, ending the dystopia without the devastation.

In the context of contemporary politics, there is little hope of emerging from dystopia anytime in the short term. Both major parties intend to maintain the surveillance culture, continue the restrictions on freedom that have been building for more than a generation, and wield the power of Leviathan against individuals who don't toe the line.

But those who remember freedom need not abandon hope. Support exists for a culture where alternative views may be voiced and heard openly and in peace. Many are weary of the military industrial complex's grip on the tiller. Many more, who want nothing more than to live at peace with their neighbors, are weary of being micromanaged by so-called leaders who think they know better. As The Powers That Be attempt to tighten the stranglehold, people still wish to come and go and they please, and to live their own lives.

We may or may not avoid the apocalypse, but many people yearn for something other than dystopia. Big Brother is an unsustainable concept. At some point totalitarianism must crumble, because despite the name its grip can never be total. The State cannot control millions and billions of individual lives against their free will. The Soviet Union collapsed. The Third Reich was a blip on history, a horrid abominable blip but gone in hardly a decade.

People get tired of living in fear. At some point they look the fear in the eye and say, "Shut up. Enough. We're going to live our lives. Try and stop us if you want, but you'll fail. Fear is not the boss of me."

The cost of freedom

Freedom is, in fact, free. We are born free. Our creator bestows freedom on us upon birth, including the right to life, liberty and the pursuit of happiness. The cost they talk about is the cost of protecting and defending those rights. There is also the cost of assuming the consequences of your free words and actions.

Who are these people who would attack your right to life, liberty and the pursuit of happiness? Well, when the phrase was coined and placed in a certain Declaration, the main culprits were a certain monarch and his minions, a king who was proclaimed the ruler over persons who lived thousands of miles from his throne room. Not surprisingly, those persons squirmed under his thumb and separated themselves from his rule.

As often happens, the ruler's response was to commit violence. Ruling by violence never wins friends, but rulers have never learned this. It's the height of arrogance to presume to rule another individual, as if the ruler knows that person's needs more intimately than the person does. But centuries and millennia have passed, and rulers still rule with threats and violence and anger and hatred.

Every so often a person tries to lead — lead, not rule — without violence but rather with love, without chains but rather with freedom, and along come the rulers to squash them. Still, their names and messages resonate through history long after their critics and killers have passed to dust. These leaders continue to be examples of hope, icons to whom we turn when we dream of a better world.

Rulers inevitably disappoint their subjects. Rulers inevitably harm their subjects. It is not human nature to be ruled or whipped into obedience, but rulers don't understand this and pull out the whips and chains and edicts and orders anyway.

Freedom is often defined as the absence of some external force. Freedom is better defined as the realization that the force has no real power and we are free to come and go as we please. Within reason, of course: No one is free to steal from or kill a neighbor, although a ruler might think he can and often does.

FULL

Without this realization that we are free, we become slaves of one sort or another. Rulers may exert ownership over our lives and property and persons, but they can never own our selves, that soul that resides in our hearts and heads. All they can do is restrict and, well, govern. But we are still free.

We can still discern right from wrong, freedom from slavery, war from peace, truth from deception, fact from fiction. They hate our freedom, but what the Creator has given, no human can fully remove. It drives them crazy, which is why so many rulers act as if they are simply insane. In fact, they are.

They can't take freedom away from us.

born free

We are born free

... and we see that other people are free, too, and everything works pretty well if we all agree we're free as long as we don't hurt others or their freedoms

... but then we start building little walls and barriers over what we can do, and then we encounter the permission-givers and who appointed them anyway

... and the little walls and barriers grow into cages, and we don't step out to test the limits as much, and so we don't realize how far we can go and we forget we're free

... and people need to encourage us to think outside the box, but the box is comfortable, so very comfortable that we forget it really doesn't exist, and we sit inside a box of our own making, free to come and go but not daring to be free

FULL

... so very comfortable that we don't see the permission-givers building a real box where the imaginary walls had been

... until it's too late.

Until it's too late?
Actually, it's almost never too late.
You've been free all along, and still are.

Remember the part where it works really well
and get back there.

Book 3
You Can Do This

FULL

a sky is full of reasons

I think a sky is full of reasons to look up.

I think there is no end to up and stars go on forever.

I think a world of possibilities is a lifetime.

I think the more I think the less I see.

I think looking up shows all the reasons to hope.

I think hope shows all the reasons to be glad.

I think glad tidings open up our heart to smile.

I think smiles in our heart can heal the world.

I think a sky is full of reasons to look up.

I think the universe wants me to see how much of it there is
    to think about,
but first it wants me to see and see and see.

Happy Monday!

Here, at the beginning, at the onset, with a clean slate, with a blank page, a new week before us, and some of us, freshly graduated or newly hired or finally retired, starting the next stage of a lifetime, with the bloom of a new day, a new week, a new season, a new year, the newness beckons.

We hear the call, re-energized, re-inspired, refreshed and renewed, as ready as we'll ever be. We know setbacks are inevitable, but for now we step forward ready for the challenge and eager to get started.

"Monday, Monday, can't trust that day"? "Blue Monday"? Ridiculous. Monday is a burst of energy. Monday is where it all begins again. Monday is a new chance to get it right this time. Monday is an opportunity to start over, the first step on a journey of a thousand miles, the day the world has been waiting for all this time, the day the ship comes in, the day the tide rolls out and clears the decks.

Happy Monday! We get to try again, or repeat what worked before, or find a new way to get it wrong and cross that one off the list of possibilities on the way to perfecting the light bulb. Every idea looks bright and shiny on Monday. Every possibility awaits to be tried and tested. Oh, what a miraculous world that has Mondays and fresh starts and opportunities and infinite possibilities!

Yes, thank God it was Friday, because the road can be hard and rocky and we need our rest, but thank God it's Monday, yes thank God I say, because see how grand is the vista before us.

It's going to be all right

It's going to be all right.

Everyone seems to be so agitated. Every day in the news and social media and everywhere we turn, someone is barking out another reason to be alarmed or horrified or, at least, offended. We live in ridiculous times.

But it's going to be all right.

I believe most of us live by an unconscious rule: We don't initiate force against other people. We don't intentionally hurt other people who haven't hurt us. Most people use force only in self-defense or in reaction to force that has been initiated against them. Otherwise, it's live and let live.

At some point it becomes clear that there's no reason to be so agitated – the person or people we're urged to hate are just folks like us, who want to live and let live. And rather than stay agitated, we turn our attention back to the things that matter – caring for family, giving neighbors a hand, living and letting live.

There will still be professional agitators out there yelling, "Look at this outrage! Be offended!"

But most people will live in peace.

And it will be all right.

Stay the course

Monday morning arrives full of energy, resolve, piss and vinegar.

Then, at the edge of consciousness, reality chips off a small piece of confidence — you start to think maybe it's not so important to get such-and-such done by 9, as long as the main job is underway by 12, and it all can't be done by 5, well, at least most of it can. But you have a nagging feeling it could have been done by 9.

Chip by chip they fall, and if enough fragments of confidence are chipped away, voila it's Tuesday and you're well along Frustration Street, which evolves into a boulevard that's one day paved over for an interstate highway.

Or you can capture the energy, bottle the resolve, tap the piss and vinegar, revive it every morning, and off you go.

Off you go!

Getting 'er done

So you want to accomplish something, but you don't have time? Of course you have.

You're awake 16 hours a day; surely you have a few minutes to spend on That Thing You Want To Do.

Even one little task is more than nothing: Put one thing on eBay. Look up how to start a business. Write 100 words of your novel. Send out one resume.

If you do that every day, you'll at minimum have put 365 things up for sale, written 36,500 words, applied for 365 jobs, by the end of the first year.

Put up a little sign where you can see it first thing: "What can I do today?" and then, before you put your head back on the pillow, do that one thing. You'll sleep better, and soon you'll see progress. Heck — Even that one thing is progress, isn't it?

Glad for a good laugh

An unexpected laugh is always on time.

I've been moving through Lucy Maud Montgomery's delightful novels about Anne Shirley Cuthbert Blythe, starting with the best-known, *Anne of Green Gables*, and following our heroine as she grows to adulthood and now motherhood.

I bought the eight-pack of paperback novels and a six-pack of audiobooks via Audible — through trying to figure out the difference, I learned that Montgomery wrote six Anne books between 1908 and 1921 and 15 years later doubled back and wrote the "fourth" book in 1936 and the "sixth" book in 1939, and the audiobooks cover the original half-dozen.

I'm reading and listening to the actual fifth book, *Rainbow Valley*, which finds Anne and her beloved Gilbert with six of the seven children they'll eventually have. We're in the early chapters, and Anne is gossiping with two old friends about the new pastor, who is a widower and the father of four precocious children of his own.

When we reach my laugh out loud, Susan Baker is telling Anne about the Reverend Meredith's daughter Faith, who is 11 when we meet. "She looks like an angel but is a holy terror for mischief," Susan says and describes what happened when a neighbor brought the Merediths a dozen eggs and a little pail of milk.

"Faith took them and whisked down the cellar with them. Near the bottom of the stairs, she caught her toe and fell the rest of the way, milk and eggs and all. You can imagine the result ... But that child came up laughing. 'I don't know whether I'm myself or a custard pie,' she said."

I honestly don't know precisely why, but Faith's reaction to her mishap produced a guffaw as I cruised down Highway 57. Anne decides she's going to like the little girl, and I'm with her.

Montgomery has a wonderful light touch in these books, and I find myself smiling — and, as you see, occasionally laughing out loud — during these visits to Prince Edward Island of a century ago. They make me want to visit P.E.I. in person someday.

Smiles and laughter are so precious, and I am grateful whenever I find them.

The fantasy that we are monsters

I'm back on Prince Edward Island in my reading, reliving The Great War with Lucy Maud Montgomery and *Rilla of Ingleside*, her sixth book featuring Anne Shirley Cuthbert Blythe of Green Gables, published in 1921. Montgomery wrote two more, prequel tales, but years later, so this will conclude her first 7-8 year burst of creativity and provide the last word chronologically on Anne and her family. Given what I've heard of the author's feelings toward war, it will not be the happiest of endings.

Are all stories, even those as whimsical as *Anne of Green Gables*, fated to grow darker as young people grow and learn more about the "realities" of the world? Or is the one who thinks the worst of humanity the one who is really living the fantasy?

We are capable of unspeakable cruelty, or there would be no wars or murders or mayhem, but our better angels call to something truly deeper and childlike within us. Our earliest natural instinct as children is to explore and learn and delight in life, before the fear and violence are trained into us. Our instinct and desire are to stay alive, to feel and enjoy this life we have. Anyone who understands that instinct in themselves is not going to wish harm or death on others.

We react violently when violence is thrust upon us, but I have to believe, left to ourselves, we mean no harm.

Perhaps I'm the foolish scientist in the old movies who doesn't want to kill the monster, only to be killed by the monster itself. I'm not so I as to suggest that monsters don't exist, but I do dare say that monsters are created, not born, and some monsters spend their time rallying our emotions to think of certain others as monsters, for the sole purpose of raising up generations of actual monsters and zombies.

How do we drive the monsters away? I am encouraged that one teaching and one teacher have resonated for more than 2,000 years: The one who taught "Love one another" and "Turn the other cheek" and forgiveness and understanding.

Somehow, from time to time, some have twisted his words into justifying the monstrous, but at the core of his life was his willingness not to strike back even at his murderers. The reason I have hope is that such a man continues to inspire the human heart at its core. If that is the core at the deepest level of our nature, we can defeat the monsters within and among us, and with love.

We risk our lives

We risk our lives
every time
we connect
in love.

We risk our lives
every time
we connect
in life.

The depth
of our love
is measured
by the depth
of our loss.

In the end,

we find,
the net gain
in our lives
is greater than the loss,

and
that buoys us
in our grief
and we begin
to heal.

Wanting to Live Forever

(Lyrics to a song I wrote Jan. 26, 1986)

I sat down this cold morning to write myself a folk song;

I sat down this cold morning to right the world's eternal
wrongs.

I wanted to write a ballad 'bout the way this cruel world
ought to be.

I wanted to write a ballad 'bout the way it is with you and
me.

I wanted to write the words so they would touch your heart
and make it melt;

I wanted to write the music so it touched you just the way I
felt,

But nothing came at all; I just got stuck on these two chords
and a phrase,

But I wanted to write so bad, I kept on going anyways.

They were words about the future and the road we travel
every day.

They were chords that flowed and grew like lovers when
they know they're gonna stay.

I had a message burning in my soul, and it cried to come out
in the song,

But it refused to give its all like lovers when they know they
don't belong.

I started to sing about how peace could come to this world in
our time;

I started to sing how killing one solitary forest is a crime;

I started to sing a melody 'bout lonely martyrs with a cause;

I started to sing how freedom means to sometimes follow
higher laws,

But a tired voice inside my heart that tingled with an
awesome sorrow,

It said, "You fool! You charlatan! No one's gonna listen to
you tomorrow.

You're a man of many failures and a man of many broken
dreams.

No one's gonna turn to you to help them sort out what all
this means.

FULL

Don't know where that voice came from, but you know? It
  kind of made me mad.
Don't know where anger comes from, but you know? It kind
  of made me glad.
'Cause it filled me with a passion, and it charged me to the
  core,
And it filled me with a reason, and it was one worth living
  for.

Listen:

It's the failures of this world that you turn around and build
  to make success.
It's the broken dreams that force you to be more when you
  could settle for less.
It's the wanting to live forever that leads you to a goal that
  will not die.
It's the wanting to see the stars that gives a simple soul the
  will to fly.

Those were words I thought might help someone to right the
  world's eternal wrongs,
So I sat down this cold morning to write myself a folk song.

The sun always sets

On the darkest day of my professional career, the universe conspired to make me laugh.

As the boss droned on about why he had sold the business to our most hated competitor, I looked down and saw the woman next to me was taking notes on a pad.

The pad had an illustration across the top of the page with the words, "One hundred years from now, none of this will matter."

Yep, I laughed, and whispered, "Thank you, Lord."

It's sort of gallows humor — after all, you know why none of our current troubles will worry us a century from now — but it has more than a kernel of truth.

Whatever's weighing you down, whatever is keeping you awake at night, even that will be over someday.

Take heart and aim for better days.

Make your escape plan

Each of us, from time to time, looks around the workaday work and thinks, "I should not be doing this. I was meant more something more or at least something else. I feel the call of the wild, the call of the pure, the art, if you will."

That's the muse whispering in your ear or bopping you upside the head. Ignore her alarm at your soul's peril.

It is foolish to skip out on your obligations to the workaday, so don't run out the door just yet. But figure out your escape plan, or at least heed the call and listen to the muse during your lunch breaks.

Jot down the skeleton of your art to flesh out later – heed the call – listen with all your heart as if it were life and death, because it is.

280

"I quit," someone said,
and maybe it was me.

But
a few minutes later
someone went back to work
and produced something
Fine.

The quitting had
cleared the air
and made way
for trying fresh.

"I quit" is not quitting;
it's pressing "reboot."

What's the point

We spend a lot of time trying to figure out what is our purpose in life. What's the meaning of "all this"?

You work your way through something day by day and sometimes try to conjure what all the somethings mean: To find a purpose, to find a story, to find a point behind it all — because we all go through life wondering what's the point? And perhaps not knowing exactly why until the story ends — At the end you tally up whether you served your purpose, or you tally up what the meaning of your life was, based on where life took you.

Who says your purpose has to be singular? An old friend of mine once said, "We each live many lifetimes within the one we live." Rather than think of it as a frustrating search for our One Big Purpose in Life, maybe we should think of it as a series of adventures trying different purposes out for size.

And maybe someday you will say "Yes, this is it, this is The Thing I Was Meant To Do." When that happens, there's no point in saying, "Oh, I'm 25 or 43 or 62 or 87 and wasted so much time getting to the point." The point is you got to the point and you're here now.

And while trying all that other stuff, surely you made an impact, and certainly that time was not wasted.

Choices we make today

A scream of consciousness cuts through the quiet: This is today, isn't it? The debris from yesterday continues to haunt, and the promises of tomorrow may or may not ring true, but today is here, right on time, to be shaped and formed now, to our pleasure and delight or to our weary horror — here and now, in any case, and ours to have and to hold.

This is today. With an ear for the echoes of yesterday and an eye for tomorrow, we hold today in our hands tightly, but not so tight that it can't be free and not so loose that it slips away.

This is the day you can make a choice, and this is the day you control your choices. Yesterday's choices are made, and tomorrow's choices have not yet presented themselves.

Today, we can choose. Today, we choose. I choose ... today. This day. This is.

The 1948 nickel

There it was, a little piece of evidence, proof that life existed before I was born. Then I realized I was surrounded by such evidence — the 1941 Philco radio, the fragile newspaper dated 1915, the Will Rogers biography from 1935 that spoke of his recent death.

What was it about the 1948 nickel that astonished me, all of a sudden? Was it the knowledge that mints minted coins years before I had a hint of what a mint was? Was it the premonition that after I am gone, the universe will continue?

The small token of years gone by reminded me how small I was but also that time's a-wasting.

I wasn't sure whether to set it aside as a constant reminder or just spend it.

46 years in the making

May 18, 1975, was a hot sunny day and my dad was proud but displeased that my college would give Bill Proxmire an honorary degree that commie and it was so hot in those black robes that somebody fainted and I don't remember any specific words that were said except "onward." And maybe nobody said "onward" but that was what they meant to say.

And 46 years have passed 46 (forty-six) [four tee sicks] are you kidding me? That's more than twice as old as I was that afternoon and so I have lived three of the lifetimes I had lived up to that moment.

Time did not fly, and it is not flying now, it is just hard to believe the planet has circled the sun 46 times since that May 18 when I stood and accepted a bit of sheepskin written in Latin because that's how traditional my college was, hard to believe because the emotions are just as fresh though long gone.

You Can Do This

I have fewer than 46 trips around the sun left and miles
to go before I sleep (or at least I hope there are miles, it could
be a few feet or a couple of inches) and so much has
happened and mistakes and triumphs and wins and losses
and pain and gain and all the rest, and here I am still to tell
the tale.

I suppose there are lessons learned and all that stuff, but
today I just remember, and — all those cliches about it feels
like only yesterday but I know it's been a long long time?
Yep. That's why it's a cliche: At some point everybody feels
it.

all these kids in caps and gowns and i remember how
they feel

A cup of coffee and a lifetime ago

I drank my first cup of coffee the morning of May 19, 1975, after successfully negotiating four years of college, including all-nighters, without the beverage.

It was the day after graduation from college. I had spent the night in an old old hotel in Waupaca, Wisconsin (I was there not long ago — Waupaca, that is, not the hotel, because I went to where it was and it wasn't anymore), and I reported as requested at 5:30 a.m. to the WDUX Radio studios on Tower Drive, where my first newscast as a professional journalist was due to be broadcast an hour later. Or wait, maybe it was two hours later, around 7:40-ish after Paul Harvey. Funny how the details blur after 46 years.

The morning man — I can see his face, but not quite his name, which is OK because it wasn't his real name, everyone had radio names then; I would be Warren Phillips for five months, chosen because Wally Phillips ruled Chicago radio at the time — said you look tired, kid, have a cup of coffee.

I don't drink coffee, I said, I never got around to it. No time like the present, he said. I poured a cup and tried it. And another. And another. And a rest-of-my-life caffeine addiction settled in.

Would my college career have been different if I'd surrendered to the coffee gods earlier? Hard to say. But waiting until that morning helped cement the fact that my new life had begun. Living in an ancient hotel until I found the apartment above the TV store a week or so later? Check. Starting my first full-time job in the adult world? Check. Drinking coffee? Check. I even attended my first Waupaca City Council meeting that night so I could experience my first 5:30 a.m. to 9 p.m. workday. Or was it 10?

I get nostalgic this time of year. WDUX recently remodeled and posted photos of its remodeled studio on Facebook, and I could see the bones of the old place in the pictures. That was the summer I bought my 12-string guitar and recorded an album's worth of songs on a Sunday afternoon in the radio station's production studio and kissed a girl shortly before midnight while "Dance With Me" was playing that time I substituted as a Saturday night DJ. I remember doing a remote broadcast from the newly opened car dealership out on the edge of town, which is now a mile or so from the edge of town because of all the development that 46 years can bring.

I only spent five months there. They never got around to raising my salary from $120 a week to $125 a week after three months like they said they would, and then the station at my adopted hometown of Ripon called and said they wanted to hire me away but could offer only $170 a week. It's one of the only times I made a career move for mercenary reasons, but it worked out well enough that I can say I lived in Ripon for 11 years, not just the four.

Sometimes we drive through Waupaca and I see what's different and what's still the same, and I wonder how my life would have evolved if I stayed. But mostly I remember a bright sunny summer and all of life ahead of me, and that first cup of coffee, and changing my name back to Warren Bluhm after introducing myself in Ripon with my radio name and having two or three people say "I thought your name was Bluhm, didn't you just graduate up at the college?" Ah, small towns.

Go For It Day

What could be different about today if you could make it so? Because, of course, you can make it so!

Do you jump out of the rut today? Is it time to commit to the future? Want to dream your biggest dream?

Look up and out at the sky — find a view where you can see it all. There's your limit.

This is a big life: Find your biggest expression of it. Don't let anyone tell you otherwise.

In praise of guilty pleasures

"Guilty pleasures" are usually defined as something not-literature or otherwise not-classy that you enjoy anyway, and it feels a little like playing hooky when you read or watch or listen to it. Where does the guilt come from?

My guilty pleasure was comic books, best of all Spider-Man and the Fantastic Four, the early days of Marvel Comics when Stan Lee and friends were just getting started. They were my gateway drugs to Nathaniel Hawthorne and Mark Twain and Emily Dickinson and George Eliot, but I digress: Even if I didn't later discover the "appropriate" classics, the Marvel stories gave me pleasure, and that fueled an eagerness to read, and that my friends is a good thing.

Read, and the world opens up to you — in fact, worlds, plural, brilliant vast worlds of possibility.

So you love detective stories or space opera or thrillers with their explosions and aliens and things that go bump in the night? So? You're reading — you're delighting in the power of these odd hieroglyphs that represent words and tell stories and pass along the wisdom of the ages.

In the film *Serenity*, a pastor's dying words are, "I don't care what you believe, just believe it." He means to say a belief in a higher power, a higher calling, anything higher — it lifts you.

I don't care what you read, just read it. And there's no need to feel guilty about the pleasure it gives you. You're connecting with another mind through words, and that is something special.

SomeOne steps forward

In the time of the great empire, when the people were hypnotized, when the air carried a hint of smoke wherever you journeyed, when birds sought shelter in concrete conclaves and rusted steel, when standing solitary to celebrate one's self was an act of bravery hated by the crowd, when despair was life's default setting ...

SomeOne sat alone, and then stood.

"May I have your attention?" SomeOne said to the crowd, which gave no attention.

"Excuse me!" SomeOne said to the crowd, which offered no excuse.

"Hey!" SomeOne shouted to the crowd, which went about its business.

"I call bullshit!" SomeOne screamed, and the crowd fell momentarily silent.

"I am SomeOne. I belong to no group, I fit no category, I reject the pigeon hole. I am unique. And so is each of you.

"I woke up this morning as SomeOne. I have always been SomeOne, but I only realized this when I woke up. I am not a demographic, I am not a generation, I am not white nor black nor other of color.

"I am SomeOne. No one in the history of humanity has been me, and no one in the future of humanity will be me. I am no one more special than another, but I am the only one. I am unique. And so are each of you.

"It is my responsibility to see each of you as who you are. Every assumption I make just looking at you is wrong. You are not your skin, you are not your age, you are not your gender – I can make no assumptions based on those things. Each of those features contributes to Who You Are, but the infinite combinations and shades of life have merged into a human being who has never ever been seen before you were born and will never ever be seen again after you die. You may think I am just like my mother, or just like my father, or just like everyone who believes something I believe, or just like everyone in my generation, or just like everyone of my gender, or just like any category you wish to put me in. I reject your categories – I am SomeOne. And so are you: You are SomeOne, too.

FULL

"The only way I can get to know you is by getting to know you. The only way you can know me is by getting to know me. I am unique. And so are you."

"Oh," someone sniffed. "It's one of *those* people." And many nodded in dismissive agreement.

But others listened to SomeOne and heard. And, one by one by one, joy began to creep back into the world.

These difficult times ain't

In the early days of the COVID-19 lockdowns, we laughed at the sixth or seventh TV ad, all of them for different products or services, all of them nearly identical, and we haven't stopped laughing.

They start with a somber solo piano ... and then the announcer says ...

"In these difficult times ..."

"We'll get through this ..."

"... because we're all in this ... together."

OK. We get the message. And I disagree.

Not with the "we'll get through this together" part. The first part.

What's so much more difficult (or "challenging" or even "unprecedented") about these times?

In fact, these times are pretty easy in comparison.

Surviving day to day has always been difficult. It's always been challenging. But modern medicine, food supply chains, communications, and a plethora of modern conveniences make surviving day to day a whole lot less difficult.

These times may be more uncomfortable than they were before someone decided that locking down the economy might be a good way to stop the spread of a serious virus (how's that working out, by the way?) — but difficult? Challenging? Unprecedented? Are you kidding me?

I'd rather be alive in 2021 than in 1941 or 1931 or 1861 or 1721 or 1621 — Now, THOSE were difficult and challenging times!

As I write this, the sun is shining, it's a mild winter day, the house is warm and comfy, and life is full of promise. I've known a lot more difficult times than this, and if you think back, I'll bet so have you.

The next time you hear somebody say those magic words, "these difficult and challenging times," laugh out loud and get back to enjoying this wonderful life.

The gift of a try

"I don't know if I can do this," you say, but the fact that you voice that thought means you're willing to try, and that's the difference.

You didn't say "I can't." You're willing to see if you can.

That's how everything moves forward: by testing your personal limits to find what you can do. More often than not, it's more than you would have expected.

You can climb that mountain after all, but first you had to say "I don't know if I can do this" and start, to see how far you could go, how much of "this" was possible, and the next thing you know is that you can do more than you knew.

"Do or do not. There is no 'try,'" Yoda said. But to try is to start doing, and when you give it a try, you often find you can finish, look back and say, "I did it. I didn't know if I could, but it was worth a try, and I discovered I could."

tomorrow

And so —

There I was.

Here I am now.

Will I be

tomorrow?

Tomorrow doesn't exist, does it?

Tomorrow there will be free beer.

Tomorrow is a

promise that may or may not be kept.

Tomorrow is Someday's evil twin sister.

Warm Breeze From Galatia

But of course, in this troubled crazy world,

The solution is to be fruit-bearing,

Fruit that is ripe and not reeking

Of the rot and decay of the age or

The lust for instant gratification.

Spirit lifters may take some time.

Is it too much to ask for a modicum of

Love that reaches past angry words and feuds,

Joy in the fullness of life everywhere,

Peace beyond the understanding of us mortals,

Patience with the process of becoming,

Kindness even toward the unkind and mean,

Goodness in the face of oncoming evil,

Faithfulness to the truths that lift us from depths,

Gentleness that turns away vicious assaults,

And, when the final victory is at hand,

Self-control to stay the course and claim the prize?

But is it done

"Don't add a line," he said. "It's perfect."

"But ..."

"Nope. Minimal, mysterious, I'm compelled."

"Shouldn't I —?"

"Nope. You said your piece. Now move on."

"But what did I say?"

"That's for your audience to decide."

"You think this will have an audience?"

"Don't worry about that yet."

"When should I worry?"

"Actually? Never. Did you say what you came to say?"

"I don't know. Kind of. Maybe."

"Then you're done here. Don't overstay your welcome."

"You think I'm welcome?"

"There you go, worrying again."

The end

This is not goodbye. This is "find me in my next book."

As long as there is breath in me, I suspect I will be trying to communicate to the outside world.

No one knows the number of his/her/their days, but I'm hoping to have breath for a while.

And so ...

I value honest feedback and would love to hear your opinion in a review, if you wish, on your favorite book retailer's site.

I blog every day at WarrenBluhm.com where most of these compositions first saw light of day.

I also have an irregular newsletter that you can join by following the link on my home page. Share your email address (I'll never re-share it) and I'll give you a freebie.

My books are available electronically via Amazon and Kobo, in paperback wherever good books are sold, and the list of books I've written or edited is growing all the time.

That list, as of now (June 2021), in more or less chronological order including the working titles of what comes next:

FULL

The Imaginary Bomb

Refuse to be Afraid

Resistance to Civil Government - Henry David Thoreau

Letters to the Citizens of the United States - Thomas Paine

A Little Volume of Secrets - James Allen, Russell H. Conwell,
 Wallace D. Wattles

A Scream of Consciousness

The Imaginary Revolution

Myke Phoenix: The Complete Novelettes

A Bridge at Crossroads

The Haunted Bookshop - Christopher Morley (Roger Mifflin
 Collection #1)

Men in War - Andreas Latzko (Roger Mifflin Collection #2)

Trivia - Logan Pearsall Smith (Roger Mifflin Collection #3)

How to Play a Blue Guitar

Gladness is Infectious

24 flashes

Full

Coming soon, Lord willing and the creek don't rise:

Jeep Thompson and The Lost Prince of Venus

Jeep Thompson and The Martian Alternative

Jeep Thompson and The World Jumpers

                              ... and then? We shall see.

FULL

INDEX

Book 1 – The Creative Soul

Book 2 – Live Free Or Die

Book 3 – You Can Do This

FULL

What are you looking back here for? This is merely the last little bit of space in the book.

What's that? The greatest wisdom may be found in the smallest and most unexpected places? True, but I'm not sure that applies here.

Still, if you hadn't looked, you never would have known.